AMAZING BLACK INVENTORS

written by
Joy James

illustrated by
Karen Dowie

Michael Terence
Publishing

— For Milton, Jade and Jules —

INTRODUCING OUR AMAZING BLACK INVENTORS...

MATTHEW CHERRY 2

KENNETH DUNKLEY 4

HENRY FAULKNER 6

LYDIA HOLMES 8

AUGUSTUS JACKSON 10

JOSEPH JACKSON (no relation to Augustus Jackson!) 12

WALLACE AMOS 14

KATHERINE JOHNSON 16

JOHN LEE LOVE 18

DEBRILLA (DEBORAH) RATCHFORD 20

LLOYD RAY 22

JOSEPH WINTERS 24

JAMES ROBINSON 26

OSBOURN DORSEY 28

JAMES FORTEN 30

MADELINE TURNER 32

MATTHEW CHERRY

How many wheels does a tricycle have?

It was invented by Matthew who added the third wheel
to stop the cycle from wobbling about
when you sat on it!

In some countries, even adults use them to carry
passengers. These are called tuktuks or rickshaws
– what great names!

Have you ridden a tricycle or bicycle,
or a tuktuk, or rickshaw?

KENNETH DUNKLEY

Have you worn 3D glasses to watch a film
at the cinema or on TV at home?

3D means three-dimensional and it makes pictures
look just like real life!

They were invented by Kenneth who was
very interested in the way that we see things!

What is your favourite film?

HENRY FAULKNER

Did you know that your feet like fresh air too?

That's why Henry made shoes with neat little holes in them so that feet could get some air and feel more comfortable — PHEW!

It can also stop blisters — OUCH! — and smelly feet — YUK!

Have you got any shoes with tiny holes in them?

LYDIA HOLMES

Do you have a toy that you can pull along by a string?

Is it made of wood?

Can you can pull it apart and build it up again?

If so, then it sounds like you have a wooden knockdown wheeled pull toy which was first made a long time ago by Lydia!

She made them in the shape of a truck or a bird or a dog!

What shape do you like best?

AUGUSTUS JACKSON

Do you like ice cream?

It helps to keep you cool on a hot day!

Augustus was a chef who loved to make fancy cakes and sweets and ice cream — YUM!

He found a better way to make ice cream and he also made lots of new and delicious ice cream recipes and flavours — YUM YUM!

What's your favourite ice cream flavour?

JOSEPH JACKSON
(no relation to Augustus Jackson!)

Imagine not having a TV remote control!
You would have to keep getting up and walking to the TV
to press the buttons on it every time you wanted to
change the channel – GROAN!

Joseph invented the remote control.
It has made life a lot easier for us all,
and probably made us all a bit lazier too...
oh dear!

What's your favourite TV show?

WALLACE AMOS

Wallace was called Wally for short and his biscuits were
called Famous Amos cookies after his surname
which rhymes nicely, doesn't it?

He became very well-known for his
giant chocolate chip cookies!

Have you eaten a really big cookie?

Can you think of any words that
rhyme with your surname?

KATHERINE JOHNSON

Katherine loved maths!

She counted EVERYTHING... the number of steps to walk to the shops... the number of plates and spoons on the table... the number of petals on flowers and so on!

She was called a 'human computer' and did amazing sums to work out how to launch rockets into space or travel around the Earth and to other planets like the Moon and Mercury — WOW!

Do you like to count?

JOHN LEE LOVE

How do you sharpen a pencil? —
with a pencil sharpener, of course!

John invented the pencil sharpener and named it after his
surname so it was called the Love sharpener!
What a LOVELY name!

Have you sharpened all your pencils?
— it helps you to write and colour better!

DEBRILLA (DEBORAH) RATCHFORD

Do you like going on holiday?

Don't pack too much in your suitcase
or it will be too heavy to carry!

Debrilla, who liked to be called Deborah, came up with the
idea of adding wheels to suitcases
to help move them easily!

Do you have another name that you like to use?

Where would you like to travel to?

LLOYD RAY

Do you help to clean your house?
It can get very messy and dirty!

Lloyd invented the dustpan, with a long handle, to make it
easier to sweep up rubbish with a broom
into the dustpan — very useful!

Some dustpans have a short handle instead!

Do you put your toys away when you've finished playing
to help keep your home nice and tidy?

JOSEPH WINTERS

Have you seen a fire engine?

They have long ladders to help firefighters put out fires in tall buildings and bring people down.

Joseph invented these ladders after finding a way of folding them up and putting them onto fire engines – what a brilliant idea!

Have you heard a fire engine?
They can be very noisy!

JAMES ROBINSON

Do you take food or drinks with you when you go out?

James made the lunchbox to help carry food and drink to work or school or on a trip. It could also help to keep food and drinks hot or cold — great idea!

What sorts of food do you to eat when you go out?
And what drinks do you like?

OSBOURN DORSEY

Imagine if your door didn't have a door knob or a door handle! How would you open it?

Thankfully, Osbourn invented the door knob to help open and close doors!
It's a very simple idea but it's a great one!

How many doors do you have in your house – can you count them?
What about all the cupboard doors too?

JAMES FORTEN

James loved ships!

He worked on a ship when he was young,
then joined the Navy and sailed the seas during wartime.

He also worked as a sailmaker and made a special type of
sail to help ships move faster in the wind!

Have you been on a ship or a boat or a raft?

Do you know any nursery rhymes?

Here is one about sailing:
"I saw a ship a sailing, a sailing on the sea!
And, oh, but it was laden, with pretty things for thee!"

MADELINE TURNER

Do you like drinking fruit juices?

Madeline invented a juicing machine or juicer to help press juice out of fruits for people to drink at breakfast time or lunchtime or dinner time or any time!

There are all kinds of juices... orange juice, apple juice, mango juice... berry juices, tropical juices and more!

What is your favourite fruit?

Acknowledgements

A huge thank you to Karen Dowie for her creative ideas and lovely illustrations.

Grateful thanks to Keith Abbott and his team at Michael Terence Publishing for their advice and help in getting this book published.

Lots of love and thanks to my wonderful family for inspiring and encouraging me on my writing journey.

About the Author

Joy James lives in London with her family. She works at a university and writes non-fiction children's books to help educate and inform curious, young minds.

She is currently working on her *Black Inventors Series*. This book is the second in this age category (0-5 years) and follows on from *Brilliant Black Inventors*.

Her first book, *101 Black Inventors and their Inventions*, is aimed at upper primary to lower secondary school ages and is followed by *Another 101 Black Inventors and their Inventions*.

First published in paperback in 2022 by Michael Terence Publishing
www.mtp.agency

ISBN 9781800944053

Copyright © 2022 Joy James

Joy James has asserted the right to be identified as the author of this work in accordance with the Copyright, Designs and Patents Act 1988

No part of this publication may be reproduced, stored in a retrieval system, or transmitted in any form or by any means, electronic, mechanical, photocopying, recording or otherwise, without the prior permission of the publisher

Illustrated by Karen Dowie

CPSIA information can be obtained
at www.ICGtesting.com
Printed in the USA
BVHW061458300922
648389BV00022B/900